HYMNS Re-Harmonized

50 FAVORITES...
with Chord Symbols!

Creative Chords for the Church Accompanist

HYMNS Re-Harmonized

50 FAVORITES...
with Chord Symbols!

Creative Chords for the Church Accompanist

Arranged by

CAROL TORNQUIST

Edited by KEN BARKER & CAROL TORNQUIST

Design by SOUTHERN DRAW DESIGN

Music Engraved by DAVID THIBODEAUX & DANNY ZALOUDIK, LIVING STONE MUSIC CO.

WORD MUSIC®

How to use HYMNS RE-HARMONIZED...

HYMNS RE-HARMONIZED was created to give church accompanists different harmonizations from those appearing in most church hymnals. I suggest that you save the "re-harmonized" version for the final verse for two reasons...

1) The singers may sing harmony (alto, tenor and/or bass) on all of the other verses. You may even want to "encourage" them ahead of time to sing unison on the last verse!

2) The lyrics are often different in final verses. (For example, AMAZING GRACE goes from "... dangers, toils and snares" to "when we've been there ten thousand years," and no one seems to sing about "...deathdew...cold on my brow" the same way they do "mansions of glory and endless delight" in the last verse of MY JESUS, I LOVE THEE.) So these re-harmonized verses often include broader, fuller accompaniment styles as well as fresh harmonies.

Each page contains chord symbols so that you may "see" the difference... as well as "hear" it! I have also included some additional "info" on pp. 106 & 107 for those who aren't used to reading chord symbols. To make it easier for you to compare (and contrast) the traditional and re-harmonized verses, I have kept them both in the same key. (However, I have included some MODULATION CHARTS (pp. 108-120) that show you how to get from any major key to another.)

Each hymn arrangement in this folio is 2 pp. long and includes:

*   INTRO... usually 2-4 bars establishing the key and tempo for the singers, using a familiar "fragment" from the melody
*   TRADITIONAL VERSE... 4-part arrangement as it appears in most church hymnals including chord symbols and lyrics of first verse
*   REPEAT ENDING... to be used as needed for additional verses
*   *Optional* TRANSITION... used as a short interlude before final verse
*   RE-HARMONIZED VERSE... last verse of hymn including chord symbols

NOTE: The second page always points out specific differences between the Traditional and Re-harmonized versions as well.

Remember that HYMNS RE-HARMONIZED was created as a resource for ACCOMPANISTS. But also remember that when it's KEYBOARD SOLOS you're looking for, check with your CBA retail store or favorite music supplier for the latest (and greatest!) keyboard solo folios available from Word Music.

"Let the Word of Christ dwell in you richly... as you sing PSALMS, HYMNS, and SPIRITUAL SONGS with gratitude in your hearts to God..."

from Colossians 3:16 (NIV)

CONTENTS

in alphabetical order

All Hail the Power of Jesus' Name
(Tune: CORONATION)

Words by
EDWARD PERRONET

Music by
OLIVER HOLDEN
Arranged by Carol Tornquist

This arrangement uses the well-known hymn tune: CORONATION. Notice that the Intro. and the Transition are identical... *except for the last bar*. In the transition (on the next page), the bar preceding the last verse uses 16th notes in the R.H. to give a more dramatic effect, signaling that this is the *final* verse.

This RE-HARMONIZED VERSE sounds *different* because:

- The first 3 bars keep "G" as the bass note *(ostinato bass)*.
- The L.H. (beginning in bar 28) has more movement and more rhythmic interest, which gives this last verse a more dramatic effect.
- The chord progression has several "surprises"... especially from bar 35 through the end.

Amazing Grace

Words by
John Newton and **John P. Rees** (stanza 5)

Traditional American melody
Arranged by Carol Tornquist

Since this classic hymn has 5 verses (at least!), the final verse definitely calls for some different harmonies! While the Intro. sounds like the last phrase of the song, notice that the Transition is completely different. (This is a welcome change since usually no verses are omitted!)

This RE-HARMONIZED VERSE sounds *different* because:

- More contemporary chords are used... *for example* Gmaj7, A9, A13, and A13+.
- There is more movement throughout the entire last verse.

America, the Beautiful

Words by
Katharine Lee Bates

Music by
Samuel A. Ward

Arranged by Carol Tornquist

Notice that the Intro. "borrows" the first 6 notes of our national anthem (*"O say, can you see..."*). They are repeated in the Transition to the last verse as well. (Actually, this beloved patriotic hymn is much easier to sing than THE STAR-SPANGLED BANNER... having brought about several attempts to have this hymn *become* our national anthem!)

This RE-HARMONIZED VERSE sounds *different* because:

- There is more movement, particularly in the inner voices.
- The harmonies change more frequently than in the traditional version.
- The final bar doesn't get back to the *tonic* chord (I) until the 3rd beat.

Angels We Have Heard on High

Traditional French carol

Traditional French melody
Arranged by Carol Tornquist

Notice that the Intro. uses *both* the chord progression *and* the familiar 8th note pattern from the chorus of this well-loved carol. While it is not *literally* the last 4 bars of the song, it definitely *suggests* the familiar refrain.

This RE-HARMONIZED VERSE sounds *different* because:

- New harmonies begin immediately on the first chord of the last verse (Fmaj7), and continue to be an interesting departure from the traditional harmonies throughout.
- Because this is the final chorus, the L.H. moves down to the lower register of the keyboard (even playing some *octaves*).

*Lyrics for last verse omitted due to lack of space.

At the Cross

Words by
Isaac Watts

Music by
Ralph E. Hudson

Arranged by Carol Tornquist

The Intro. is based on a *combination* of the first two bars of the chorus (*"At the cross, at the cross where I first saw the light..."*) and the last two bars (*"...And now I am happy all the day"*). These well-known melodic fragments let the singers know for sure which hymn they are about to sing. Notice that although the melody is familiar, the harmonies are not... which adds musical "fresh air" from the very first note!

This RE-HARMONIZED VERSE sounds *different* because:

- There is a lot of movement in the inner voices (mostly *passing tones*).
- The chords change more frequently than in the traditional version.
- Many "altered" chords are used (usually indicated by the use of *accidentals...* or notes not found in the key of E♭.)

Be Thou My Vision

Traditional Irish hymn

Traditional Irish melody
Arranged by Carol Tornquist

The melody of this beautiful hymn tune is introduced by using the first part of the third line *("Thou my best thought...")*.
With the renewed interest in Irish music, this hymn has been *rediscovered* in some churches... and has broad appeal in both
traditional and contemporary forms of worship. Notice how similar the Transition is to the Intro.

This RE-HARMONIZED VERSE sounds *different* because:

- Many contemporary chords are used... especially major and minor 7s and 9s.
- The bass line generally moves by just a *whole step* or a *half step* (which it also did in the traditional version). However, the actual chords don't change as often, particularly in the first half of the final verse.

Beneath the Cross of Jesus

Words by
ELIZABETH C. CLEPHANE

Music by
FREDERICK C. MAKER
Arranged by Carol Tornquist

Because this hymn is in the key of D♭ Major, several double flats (♭♭) are used. Don't let that intimidate you, though! (Just remember to play them *one half-step lower* than "regular" flats.) Notice that the Intro. is *loosely* based on the last 4 bars.

This RE-HARMONIZED VERSE sounds *different* because:

- Several "altered" chords are used (which means even *more accidentals* than in the first verse)!
- The very last bar of this final verse uses a single note... the *tonic* (D♭)... before adding the harmony beneath it on the second and third beats. This gives it a more dramatic effect because it signals the "end," and should include a *ritard*.

Blessed Assurance

Words by
FANNY J. CROSBY

Music by
PHOEBE P. KNAPP

Arranged by Carol Tornquist

This hymn favorite is notated in *compound meter*, meaning that the notes that get the "beat" (8th notes) are in groups of 3. The "9" in the time signature tells you that there are 9 beats/measure... although, at a moderately fast tempo, it "feels" like the song has 3 beats/measure... or 3 *groups of* 3! Incidentally, in $\frac{9}{8}$ time a 2 bar Intro. is often enough to establish the "feel" of a song. (You will notice that most songs in this folio are in *simple meter*, and have 4 bar Intros.)

This RE-HARMONIZED VERSE sounds *different* because:

- There is a lot more movement... especially in the L.H. The rhythm pattern (♩ ♪) is used to give it "energy." (Notice that the first verse L.H. used mostly dotted quarter notes.)
- More contemporary harmonies are included... *for example*, major 7s and 9s, minor 7s and "altered" chords.

Break Thou the Bread of Life

Words by
MARY A. LATHBURY

Music by
WILLIAM F. SHERWIN
Arranged by Carol Tornquist

The Intro. is taken from the first phrase of the verse using chords similar to the re-harmonized verse. Notice that bar 4 uses Em7/A rather than the more traditional dominant (A or A7). The same harmony (Em7/A) has been added to the first ending as an aid to the singers. (And remember... this is *not* a communion hymn!)

This RE-HARMONIZED VERSE sounds *different* because:

• Traditional harmonies are enhanced by substituting major 7s and 9s (e.g. Dmaj7 and Gmaj9) as well as minor 7s and 9s (e.g. Em7 and Am9).
• Once again, moving inner voice parts add *fullness* and *flow* to the music. (Compare bars 32-38 to bars 11-17 on the previous page.)

Christ the Lord Is Risen Today

Words by
CHARLES WESLEY

Lyra Davidica, 1708
Arranged by Carol Tornquist

Surely the most well-known Easter song of all, this hymn celebrating Christ's resurrection should always be played with *energy*! Even though the Intro. doesn't use the "note for note" melody, there is no doubt which hymn is about to be sung because of the R.H. rhythm established in the first 2 measures (♩♪♪♪♪ ♪ ♩). By the time the congregation hears the familiar melody of *"Al-le-"* (*lu-ia*) in the third measure, they should be ready to join you (with "gusto") on the first note of the first verse!

Arr. © Copyright 2000 Word Music, Inc.
All rights reserved.

This RE-HARMONIZED VERSE sounds *different* because:

- There are lots of harmonic "surprises" (particularly since this hymn is so familiar)!
- In the last half of this final verse the L.H. begins to play in *octaves* until the last *"alleluia."* This provides more fullness for the voices as they approach the triumphant end of the hymn. (Don't forget the *ritard* in the last two measures!)

Come, Thou Long-Expected Jesus

(Tune: Hyfrydol)

Words by
Charles Wesley

Music by
Rowland H. Prichard

Arranged by Carol Tornquist

Because of the time signature and the moderately fast tempo of this familiar hymn tune, it seems to need a full 8 bar Intro.
Notice that the chord progression is taken from the *re-harmonized* verse rather than the traditional one.

This RE-HARMONIZED VERSE sounds *different* because:

- Chords don't always change as often as in the traditional harmonization.
- The L.H. bass line is more fluid (moving more by *step* than *skip*).

Come, Ye Thankful People, Come

Words by
Henry Alford

Music by
George J. Elvey

Arranged by Carol Tornquist

Notice that the Intro. merely "suggests" both the melody and the rhythm of the first 2 bars of this familiar Thanksgiving hymn.

This RE-HARMONIZED VERSE sounds *different* because:

- There is more movement in: inner voices, R.H. melody and L.H. accompaniment.
- The more contemporary harmonies add *subtle* interest to this traditional melody without taking it too far from the original (and out of context).

Crown Him with Many Crowns

(Tune: DIADEMATA)

Words by
MATTHEW BRIDGES

Music by
GEORGE J. ELVEY
Arranged by Carol Tornquist

This well-known hymn is introduced by using the first 6 notes of the melody, which should be played like a "fanfare" (*accented!*) The Intro. ends with the A7 (*dominant 7*) chord... a strong lead-in to the *tonic* (D) at the beginning of the verse. Notice that the A7 chord is used again in the first ending for additional repeats. The R.H. repeated "D" (♩. ♫ ♩) adds to the *majesty* of this stately hymn. Notice that the Transition sounds fuller than the Intro. because of the added L.H. octaves.

This RE-HARMONIZED VERSE sounds *different* because:

- The chord inversions are more interesting due to the L.H. octaves which move mostly in *whole* or *half steps*.
- The R.H. rhythm pattern from the first ending (♩. ♪♩ ♩) is used again in this final verse, which adds musical continuity to the arrangement. (See bars 29, 33, 35, 37, and 41.)

Fairest Lord Jesus

Anonymous German hymn

Schlesische Volkslieder
Arranged by Carol Tornquist

Even though the Intro. is a departure from the original harmonization (and uses more 8th notes!), make sure that you play it *evenly* and *legato* (smoothly). It will add to the "elegant simplicity" of this classic hymn.

This RE-HARMONIZED VERSE sounds *different* because:

- There is more movement in both hands.
- When played at a somewhat *slower tempo* than the previous verses... and *forte* rather than mezzo-forte... these more interesting harmonies will add to the drama of the lyric which moves from "pictures" of nature (e.g. meadows, sunshine, and the garb of spring) to praising the Lord of creation forever and ever!

Grace Greater than Our Sin

Words by
Julia H. Johnston

Music by
Daniel B. Towner
Arranged by Carol Tornquist

Although the Intro. is based on the last phrase of the chorus, bars 3 and 4 use C/D and D7 leading into the first verse... which gives it more musical interest than *literally* playing the last 4 bars!
The Transition is then based on the Intro. (with the addition of some different chords and octaves in the R.H.).

This RE-HARMONIZED VERSE sounds *different* because:

- The R.H. uses more *octaves.*
- Several altered chords are used.
- The L.H. has more of a *broken chord style* of accompaniment in the refrain.

*Lyrics for last verse omitted due to lack of space.

Hark! the Herald Angels Sing

Words by
CHARLES WESLEY

Music by
FELIX MENDELSSOHN

Arranged by Carol Tornquist

The familiar "device" of using the last four bars of the song as an intro. is used in this familiar carol. The very first bar sounds more like a "fanfare" by omitting the L.H., and makes musical sense with the lyric: *"Hark"*!

This RE-HARMONIZED VERSE sounds *different* because:

- The bass line moves more by *step* than by using larger intervals *(skips)*.
- There is much more movement in the inner voices (especially in bars 38, 40, and 42).
- The fuller accompaniment style for this final verse works well with the "drama" of the lyrics. (Be sure to bring out the moving bass line in the last 8 bars.)

Have Thine Own Way, Lord

Words by
ADELAIDE A. POLLARD

Music by
GEORGE C. STEBBINS
Arranged by Carol Tornquist

The following hymn is notated in *compound meter*, meaning the notes that get the "beat" (quarter notes) are in groups of 3. The time signature ($\frac{9}{4}$) tells you that there are 9 beats/measure and the quarter note gets one beat.

This RE-HARMONIZED verse sounds *different* because:

- The L.H. part has more movement.
- The bass line is more interesting due to the use of *chord inversions*.
- The R.H. part has a lot of movement in the inner voices (including several *passing tones*).
- The harmonies are less predictable than in the traditional version.

He Leadeth Me

Words by
Joseph Gilmore

Music by
William B. Bradbury
Arranged by Carol Tornquist

Notice that the Intro. repeats the first 4 melody notes of the verse (*"He leadeth me..."*), but changes the underlying harmony from C Major (bar 1) to Am (bar 2) to Fmaj7 (bar 3). This repeated melodic fragment tells the singers which hymn they are about to sing!

This RE-HARMONIZED VERSE sounds *different* because:

- The L.H. uses more notes in the *lower register* than in the traditional hymn.
- Instead of there being a *fermata* ("hold") at the end of each 4 bar phrase, a $\frac{2}{4}$ bar is included. This feels "natural" and takes the rhythmic "guesswork" out of your job! (NOTE: You'll want to play the previous verses using *exactly the same rhythm* for congregational singing.)

His Eye Is on the Sparrow

Words by
CIVILLA P. MARTIN

Music by
CHARLES H. GABRIEL
Arranged by Carol Tornquist

This hymn is often used as a solo, so the verse is sometimes sung more *freely* than in most hymns. However, the chorus definitely has 6 beats/measure, and is usually sung at a higher dynamic level than the verses because of the "happy" lyrics. The Intro. sets the tone for the verse, and may be played rather freely (depending on how your congregation happens to know the song). Notice that the Transition is only two bars long.

This RE-HARMONIZED VERSE sounds *different* because:

- There are many altered chords and more movement in the L.H.

*Lyrics for last verse omitted due to lack of space.

Holy, Holy, Holy! Lord God Almighty

Words by
REGINALD HEBER

Music by
JOHN B. DYKES

Arranged by Carol Tornquist

The chord progression of the Intro. is based on the last phrase of the re-harmonized verse, and is repeated (with slight variations) in the Transition. Notice that the measure immmediately preceding the final verse has an *ascending major scale* in the R.H. which should be played with a *crescendo*. A *rallentando* is also suggested to give the last verse a broader feel. (Notice that except for the third line, the lyrics for the first and last verses are exactly the same, giving added *emphasis* to verse 4.)

This RE-HARMONIZED VERSE sounds *different* because:

• The R.H. is played an *octave higher* in fuller 4 note chords.
• The L.H. adds more movement.
• Some additional *passing tones* have been added to the R.H. leading to the next melody note. (NOTE: It is important that these notes simply "round out" the arrangement, not create dissonance for the singers.)

I Am Thine, O Lord

Words by
Fanny J. Crosby

Music by
William H. Doane

Arranged by Carol Tornquist

The last phrase of this familiar chorus *("draw me nearer . . .")* becomes the 4 bar Intro. The Transition to the last verse is only 2 bars long, ending with a *diminished* chord. This is a bit unusual, but works well since the first chord of the verse is G/A.

This RE-HARMONIZED VERSE sounds *different* because:

• The chords are much more varied than in the traditional version which is mostly based on the tonic (I), subdominant (IV) and dominant (V, V7).
• The chords change more frequently and often appear as inversions.

In My Heart There Rings a Melody

Words and Music by
ELTON M. ROTH
Arranged by Carol Tornquist

The Intro. uses the familiar melody from the chorus of this joyful hymn. The Transition begins the same as the Intro., but then adds a "playful" ascending scale (using ♪♪) going into the final verse.

This RE-HARMONIZED VERSE sounds *different* because:

- Some *triplets* ( ) are added. Remember that the whole song should have a *triplet feel* (i.e. =). This rhythmic indication is found in many gospel music publications, and has a more "relaxed" feel than strict dotted 8ths and 16ths.
- Due to the nature of this song, the arrangement should be played in a light (and "fun") style!

In the Garden

Words and Music by
C. AUSTIN MILES

Arranged by Carol Tornquist

Don't forget that this beloved hymn is in *compound meter* (8th notes in groups of 3 rather than 2). Also, there are 6 beats/measure because the tempo is slower than most songs in this meter. By using 8th notes, the Intro. establishes the "flowing" feel of a slow $\frac{6}{8}$ meter rather than giving the listener melodic "clues" (as in most introductions).

This RE-HARMONIZED VERSE sounds different because:

- There is a lot of movement in the inner voices.
- More contemporary harmonies are used (e.g. major and minor 7s, 13s, and flat 9s).
- The L.H. has more rhythmic interest, *for example* often using the rhythmic pattern ♪♩♪.

It Is Well with My Soul

Words by
HORATIO G. SPAFFORD

Music by
PHILIP P. BLISS

Arranged by Carol Tornquist

The Intro. for this beloved hymn borrows from the melody in a more "subtle" way than usual. Notice that the notes having a stress mark over the note head are taken from: *". . . peace like a river attend . . ."*. These R.H. 8th notes should be played smoothly *(legato)*... like flowing water! The Transition is very similar to the Intro., and should be played at a louder dynamic level to prepare for the dramatic lyrics of the final verse.

This RE-HARMONIZED VERSE sounds *different* because:

• The R.H. is played an *octave higher* in the verse, using full 4 note chords.
• The L.H. adds both movement and fullness by playing several 8th note *arpeggios.*
• In the chorus, the "echo" part is filled in with the R.H. 8th note keyboard part. Also, the end of the last verse includes an extra measure which sounds like an instrument echo of the last 3 words: *". . . with my soul".*

Jesus Loves Me

Words by
ANNA B. WARNER

Words and Music by
WILLIAM B. BRADBURY

Arranged by Carol Tornquist

Of all the hymns in *any* hymnal, this one probably "bridges the generation gap" more effectively (and more universally) than any other! In the Intro. the familiar melody of the lyric *"Jesus loves me"* is repeated in measures 1, 2, and 3 with different chord structures each time. This musical repetition is called a *sequence*. Notice that the Transition (unlike the Intro.) is only 2 bars long (repeating the last phrase of the chorus).

This RE-HARMONIZED VERSE sounds *different* because:

- Many altered chords are used.
- More chord *inversions* are used, allowing for a more flowing bass line. (The traditional harmonization uses mostly "root position" chords.)
- There is more movement in both the L.H. and the inner voices.

Jesus Paid It All

Words by
Elvina M. Hall

Music by
John T. Grape

Arranged by Carol Tornquist

This arrangement retains the *simplicity* of this reflective hymn. The Intro. borrows the well-known melody of the chorus, and is repeated as the Transition. Notice that the chords used in the Intro. and the Transition are different from *both* the traditional and re-harmonized versions.

This RE-HARMONIZED VERSE sounds *different* because:

• More *chord inversions* are used.
• More movement in the inner voices adds interest.

NOTE: Because this hymn has 5 flats in the key signature, it was necessary to use some double flats (
) in the notation of this
verse. (Just remember to make it an *extra half step lower!*)

Joy to the World!

Words by
ISAAC WATTS

Music by
G. F. HANDEL

Arranged by Carol Tornquist

This familiar Christmas/Advent carol is one of the few songs in the hymnal with a time signature of 2/4. The Intro. begins with a familiar melodic "fragment" from the last phrase *("...heav'n and heav'n")*. The Transition is similar to the Intro., but changes harmony in the second measure. Notice that the R.H. *ascending major scale* in the second ending "signals" the Transition to the final verse.

This RE-HARMONIZED VERSE sounds *different* because:

- The L.H. is playing in a *lower register* of the keyboard.
- The L.H. *octaves* give strength to the lyrics: *"He rules the world..."*.
- The R.H. is much fuller as well, often using 4 note chords.

Joyful, joyful, We Adore Thee

(Hymn to joy)

Words by
Henry van Dyke

Music by
Ludwig van Beethoven

Arranged by Carol Tornquist

The Intro. to this familiar hymn begins on the *upper register* of the keyboard, which makes perfect sense with the "joyful" sound of this timeless melody. The Transition, however, (which also borrows from the last phrase of the song) uses L.H. descending octaves to lead into the more dramatic lyrics of the final verse. (Since the last verse is usually sung at a somewhat slower, broader tempo, you should observe the *rallentando* in bars 24 and 25.)

This RE-HARMONIZED VERSE sounds *different* because:

- The L.H. includes several octaves.
- The L.H. often moves in *half* and *whole steps*. (Notice that in the traditional harmonization many of the bass notes are repeated instead.)

Just As I Am

Words by
CHARLOTTE ELLIOTT

Music by
WILLIAM B. BRADBURY

Arranged by Carol Tornquist

This familiar "invitation" hymn is the only song in this book with a time signature of $\frac{6}{4}$. It is also the only arrangement that includes an Intro. with 3 bars . . . just like the last phrase of the song. Notice that both endings have some added L.H. movement . . . otherwise the Db Major chord would be held for 6 beats!

This RE-HARMONIZED VERSE sounds *different* because:

• The chords change much more frequently than in the traditional version.
• The movement in the inner voices adds harmonic interest as well.
• Several altered chords have been added, giving the final verse a more contemporary sound.

Lead On, O King Eternal

Words by
ERNEST W. SHURTLEFF

Music by
HENRY T. SMART

Arranged by Carol Tornquist

This hymn is often used at the end of a worship service as we "go out into the world". The L.H. octaves in the very first bar of this Intro. set a "strong" tone for the entire song. The Transition expands upon the Intro., adding some R.H. 16th notes as a sort of "fanfare" into the final verse.

This RE-HARMONIZED VERSE sounds *different* because:

• More contemporary harmonies are used.
• The L.H. part has much more interest than the traditional version, both rhythmically and harmonically.

Leaning on the Everlasting Arms

Words by
Elisha A. Hoffman

Music by
Anthony J. Showalter

Arranged by Carol Tornquist

Although this uptempo hymn is notated in $\frac{4}{4}$ time, it "feels" like $\frac{12}{8}$ ... or *triplet feel* throughout (as indicated by: ♪♪ = ♪ ♪).
That rhythm is well established in the Intro., especially in the L.H. The Transition is a repeat of the Intro. (except for bar 25).

This RE-HARMONIZED VERSE sounds *different* because:

• By using several chord inversions the L.H. can move naturally by *whole* and *half steps* (rather than by larger intervals as in the traditional version).
• More contemporary chords are used . . . *for example,* major chords with an added "2" and major and minor 7s.
• The L.H. definitely helps to keep the triplet feel throughout.

Let Us Break Bread Together

Traditional Spiritual
Arranged by Carol Tornquist

This traditional spiritual is probably the most familiar communion hymn of all. Even though the time signature is $\frac{4}{4}$, it is often sung in "cut time" (2 beats/measure).

This RE-HARMONIZED VERSE sounds *different* because:

• The melody of the first phrase is played an *octave higher* . . . which "fits" because the lyrics have changed from *"breaking bread"* and *"drinking the cup"* to *"praising God."*
• The ascending bass line in that first phrase gives a *legato* (connected) feel to the arrangement.
• Adding notes to the triads (like 9s, 11s and 13s) gives the harmony a richer sound.

My Jesus, I Love Thee

Words by
William R. Featherston

Music by
Adoniram J. Gordon

Arranged by Carol Tornquist

The familiar melodic fragment in this Intro. is taken from bars 13 and 14 (*". . . my gracious Redeemer . . ."*). The Transition has a fuller sound (due to L.H. octaves) and a *rall.* to signal the broader final verse: *"In mansions of glory . . ."*.

This RE-HARMONIZED VERSE sounds *different* because:

- The tempo is broader to enhance the lyrics.
- The L.H. is played in a *lower* (and stronger) register of the keyboard, using several *octaves*.
- The bass line is more "fluid" (often moving by *whole* or *half steps*) because more *chord inversions* are used.

My Savior's Love

Words and Music by
CHARLES H. GABRIEL

Arranged by Carol Tornquist

The familiar chorus: *"How marvelous! How wonderful!"* clearly "sets the stage" for this well-known hymn about God's love for us. The harmonization for the Intro. is repeated in the final chorus.

This RE-HARMONIZED VERSE sounds *different* because:

• The additional movement (L.H. and inner voices) gives *energy* to this final verse and chorus when the lyrics speak of our *eternal hope in Christ.*
• Several chords are a real departure from the traditional ones, but don't seem contrived (or out of place) . . . especially since the lyrics are also a departure from previous verses.

Near the Cross

Words by
FANNY J. CROSBY

Music by
WILLIAM H. DOANE

Arranged by Carol Tornquist

Because this hymn is in $\frac{6}{8}$ meter, a 2 bar Intro. is sufficient to establish the rhythmic feel for the singers. You will notice that several arrangements in this folio repeat part of the Intro. as the Transition. In this one, however, the Transition borrows from the melody of the last phrase of the song, and moves naturally into the final verse.

This RE-HARMONIZED VERSE sounds *different* because:

- There is movement *on every beat* (in this case, 6/measure) . . . in the inner voices, the L.H. or both.
- As in other arrangements, the use of chord inversions makes a *legato* bass line possible.
- The R.H. sometimes "embellishes" the melody without confusing or distracting the singers.

Nothing but the Blood

Words and Music by
ROBERT LOWRY

Arranged by Carol Tornquist

The Intro. to this hymn once again utilizes the last phrase of this well-known chorus. Because the traditional harmonization consists only of the three *primary chords* (I, IV and V or V7 . . . G, C and D or D7), both you and the singers will be ready for something more adventuresome by the final verse!

This RE-HARMONIZED VERSE sounds *different* because:

- The chords are "fuller" . . . *for example,* there are several 4 note chords (like major and minor 7s and 9s).
- Many more *chord inversions* are used than in the traditional version where every single chord is played in root position!
- The L.H. has more movement, especially in the chorus.

O Come, All Ye Faithful
(Adeste Fidelis)

Latin Hymn

Music by
JOHN FRANCIS WADE

Arranged by Carol Tornquist

Here are some new harmonic ideas for a carol you will be playing over and over again this (and every!) Christmas season. Notice that while the Intro. does use the familiar last phrase of the chorus, the chord progression is different from the traditional version. The same chord progression then serves as an *interlude* (Transition) preceding the final verse with minor changes in bar 29 for dramatic effect.

This RE-HARMONIZED VERSE sounds *different* because:

• Many altered chords are used (indicated by several *accidentals*).
• The L.H. bass line moves smoothly (often by *whole* or *half steps*), made possible by the use of *chord inversions*.
• There is more movement in the L.H., especially in the chorus.

O Come, O Come, Emmanuel

Latin hymn

Adapted from Plainsong
by Thomas Helmore
Arranged by Carol Tornquist

This ancient tune is probably the most widely used Advent carol. (Some hymnals include as many as 8 verses, so some re-harmonization is definitely a welcome change!) Notice that while the verse is in a minor key (E minor), the chorus sounds as though it is in the *relative major* key of G major (same key signature 3 half steps higher). This "major" sound fits the lyrics: *"Rejoice! Rejoice!"*

This RE-HARMONIZED VERSE sounds *different* because:

- The first chord is Cmaj7 *rather than the tonic* (Em).
- More contemporary harmonies have been added (e.g. Am7, Am9, C2, Cmaj7 and Cmaj9).
- The L.H. part is much more interesting, especially in the chorus.
- The final chord is *major* rather than *minor*... since the chorus says: *"Rejoice"*!

Only Trust Him

Words and Music by
jOHN H. STOCKTON

Arranged by Carol Tornquist

The open 3 note harmony in the first 2 measures of the Intro. seems to fit the beautiful simplicity of this hymn. Notice that the more "lush" harmony used in the Transition prepares the listeners for the final verse harmonization.

This RE-HARMONIZED VERSE sounds *different* because:

- The melody of the entire verse is played an *octave higher* . . . fitting the confident lyrics: *("Yes, Jesus is the Truth, the Way . . .")*.
- The L.H. moves *smoothly*, often by half and whole steps, creating a "flowing" bass line. (By contrast, the verse used several repeated bass notes.)
- The chords are much richer and fuller, including minor 7s, minor 6s, *diminished* and *augmented* chords.

Pass Me Not

Words by
Fanny J. Crosby

Music by
William H. Doane

Arranged by Carol Tornquist

While this Intro. uses the "predictable" last phrase of the song, the subtle difference in the harmony and R.H. rhythm in bar 3 adds a more contemporary sound. Notice that the 2 bar Transition simply repeats the last half of the last phrase *(. . . do not pass me by")*.

This RE-HARMONIZED VERSE sounds *different* because:

- Several augmented and minor 7 chords are used.
- The L.H. has a lot more movement, especially in the chorus . . . which helps to enhance the intensity of the lyrics.

Redeemed

Words by
FANNY J. CROSBY

Music by
WILLIAM J. KIRKPATRICK

Arranged by Carol Tornquist

Notice how the meter of this great hymn ($\frac{6}{8}$) "fits" the joyful lyrics! (Remember that a moderately fast $\frac{6}{8}$ *feels* like
2 beats/measure!) Once again, the Intro. uses both familiar melodic fragments and rhythms to "set the stage" for the singers.

This RE-HARMONIZED VERSE sounds *different* because:

• The fresh harmonies add interest without straying too far from the traditional version.
• The inner voices moving *stepwise* help to "drive" the last verse.

Rock of Ages

Words by
AUGUSTUS M. TOPLADY

Music by
THOMAS HASTINGS

Arranged by Carol Tornquist

The first phrase of this familiar hymn becomes the Intro. Even though the entire song is only 12 bars long, it has surely stood the "test of time" to become a classic of the church! Notice that the Transition expands upon the second half of the Intro.

This RE-HARMONIZED VERSE sounds *different* because:

• The very first chord is *augmented* (raised 5th).
• The use of *chord inversions* helps to achieve a smoother bass line than in the traditional version (which sometimes *jumps* from one root position chord to another).
• The traditional harmonization uses basically the I, IV and V chords in the key of Bb Major (Bb, Eb and F) . . . while the final verse substitutes IIm7 (Cm7), VIm7 (Gm7) *and more*!

Savior, Like a Shepherd Lead Us

Hymns for the Young
attr. to Dorothy A. Thrupp

Music by
WiLLiAM B. BRADBURY

Arranged by Carol Tornquist

The gentle feel of this hymn is introduced by using the *upper register* of the keyboard in the first measure. In the Transition, however, the melody remains in the middle register, although it is nearly identical otherwise to the Intro.

This RE-HARMONIZED VERSE sounds *different* because:

• It begins with a major 7 chord going to a minor 9, which instantly tells you that the harmonic structure is more contemporary in nature. Notice that the first verse is based for the most part on D, G and A (or A7) . . . or the *tonic*, *subdominant* and *dominant* (or *dominant seventh*).

• The melody is sometimes "embellished" without being confusing or distracting to the singers.

LAST VERSE

4. Ear - ly let us seek Thy fa - vor;____ Ear - ly let us do Thy will;

Bless - ed Lord and on - ly Sav - ior,____ With Thy love our be - ings fill: Bless - ed

Je - sus, bless - ed Je - sus, Thou hast loved us, love us still; Bless - ed

Je - sus, bless - ed Je - sus, Thou hast loved us, love us still.

Silent Night! Holy Night!

Words by
JOSEPH MOHR

Music by
FRANZ GRÜBER

Arranged by Carol Tornquist

The Intro. begins with the first notes of the last phrase: *"Sleep in . . .",* then repeats them an octave lower in the second bar (which is in the actual vocal range of the singers). Because of the slow tempo, there really are 6 beats/measure in this classic carol.

This RE-HARMONIZED VERSE sounds *different* because:

• The first 2 bars are played an *octave higher*. (Compare the harmonization in these 2 bars with the first verse. Even though the "root" of each chord is B, adding the major 7 and the 6 is much more interesting than simply using the I chord for 2 entire measures!)
• The L.H. rhythm (♪♩♪) adds movement to this final verse.

Softly and Tenderly

Words and Music by
WiLL L. THOMPSON
Arranged by Carol Tornquist

The melody notes for *"...Calling, 'O sinner...'"* are repeated in the first 3 bars of the Intro. to this familiar hymn of invitation. (The Transition then borrows only the 3rd measure.) Notice how the R.H. ascending major scale in bar 23 gives the singers their vocal cue for the final verse.

This RE-HARMONIZED VERSE sounds *different* because:

- Many altered chords are used.
- The harmonies change more frequently.
- There is more movement both in the L.H. and the inner voices.

The Old Rugged Cross

Words and Music by
GEORGE BENNARD

Arranged by Carol Tornquist

Instead of using the last phrase of this hymn classic as an Intro., the *first* phrase of the chorus is used *("...so I'll cherish the old rugged cross").* Notice that this same melody is used in the Transition, but with different harmonization (Cm = C and F7 = Ebm).

This RE-HARMONIZED VERSE sounds *different* because:

- A lot of movement is added to the inner voices as well as the L.H.
- The chords change more frequently.

*Lyrics for last verse omitted due to lack of space.

There Is a Fountain

Words by
WILLIAM COWPER

Traditional American melody
Arranged by Carol Tornquist

This Intro. begins with the familiar melody which is found 3 times within this hymn (bars 11-12, 13-14 and 19-20). The Transition is based on the second half of the Intro.

This RE-HARMONIZED VERSE sounds *different* because:
- Many altered chords are used [in contrast with the first verse, which uses mainly the 3 *primary chords*: Bb, Eb and F (7).]
- Some *embellishments* have been added to the R.H. melody, but are never distracting or confusing to the singers.

To God Be the Glory

Words by
FANNY J. CROSBY

Music by
WILLIAM H. DOANE

Arranged by Carol Tornquist

The Intro. of this arrangement is quite simple which makes sense with the basic harmonies of the first verse. Notice that the melody of the Transition *ascends* (rather than descends, as in the Intro.) giving an extra "lift" to the final verse.

This RE-HARMONIZED VERSE sounds *different* because:

• The chords change more often than in the traditional version.
• More chord inversions are used.
• The bass line is definitely more interesting! (Note ascending bass line... bar 67 through 71.)

Were You There?

Traditional Spiritual
Arranged by Carol Tornquist

This traditional spiritual is widely used during Lent and often as a vocal solo. Even the traditional harmonization is more interesting than many hymns, using several chord inversions. (See measures 9, 12 and 13, *for example*.)

This RE-HARMONIZED VERSE sounds *different* because:

• More contemporary chords are used . . . for example major 2s, 7s and 9s, minor 7s and augmented chords (+).
• The verse begins with the melody an *octave higher* and moving 8ths in the L.H. That's because the text changes from *crucifixion* and *burial* in verses 1-3 to the *resurrection* in verse 4!

What Child Is This?

Words by
WILLIAM C. DIX

Traditional English melody
Arranged by Carol Tornquist

Notice that the rhythm of the Intro. is "busier" than the first verse, but creates a strong $\frac{6}{8}$ meter by the time the singers enter at bar 5. The Transition is played an *octave higher* using 6ths in the R.H.

This RE-HARMONIZED VERSE sounds *different* because:

• The A9 chord in the first measure is the listener's first "clue" that this harmonization will be a departure from the traditional!
• The L.H. movement adds "energy" to this final verse, enhancing the lyrics.

Chord Symbols

The following chord symbols are included for those accompanists whose musical background emphasized "reading what was on the page" more than understanding music theory and harmony. The key of C Major is used as a "model" on the following 2 pages, *but the same "rules" apply in any major key.*

TYPES OF CHORDS*	CHORD SYMBOL
MAJOR (letter name only)	C
MINOR (letter name plus 'm')	Cm
AUGMENTED (letter name plus '+')	C+ (or C aug.)
AUGMENTED SEVEN (letter name plus '+7')	C+7 (or C aug.7)
DIMINISHED (letter name plus '°')	C° (or C dim.)
DIMINISHED SEVEN (letter name plus '°7')	C°7 (or C dim.7)
SUSPENDED (letter name plus 'sus')	Csus
SUSPENDED 4,2 (letter name plus 'sus $\frac{4}{2}$')	Csus $\frac{4}{2}$
MAJOR WITH ADDED 2 (letter name plus '2')	C2
MAJOR WITH ADDED 6 (letter name plus '6')	C6
DOMINANT SEVEN (letter name plus '7')	C7
NINE (letter name plus '9')	C9
DOMINANT SEVEN SUSPENDED (letter name plus '7 sus')	C7sus
DOMINANT SEVEN FLAT NINE (letter name plus '7b9')	C7b9
MINOR SIX (letter name plus 'm6')	Cm6
MINOR SEVEN (letter name plus 'm7')	Cm7
MINOR SEVEN FLAT FIVE (letter name plus 'm7b5')	Cm7b5
MINOR SEVEN WITH ADDED FOUR (letter name plus 'm7(4)')	Cm7(4)
MAJOR SEVEN (letter name plus 'maj7')	Cmaj7
MAJOR NINE (letter name plus 'maj9')	Cmaj9
NINE SUSPENDED (letter name plus '9sus')	C9sus
THIRTEEN (letter name plus '13')	C13

*NOTE: These are most of the *standard* chords used in church music (and in this folio) . . . but there are many others not included here!

The notation for 22 of the standard chord symbols appears below. Each chord may, of course, be *voiced* in more than one way. (In fact, all of the RE-HARMONIZED verses in this book include several *chord inversions*.)

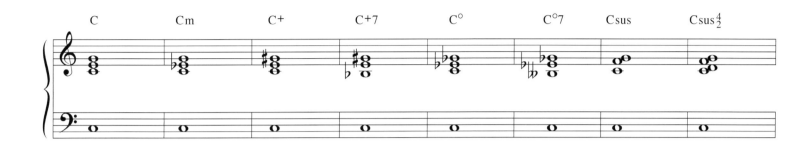

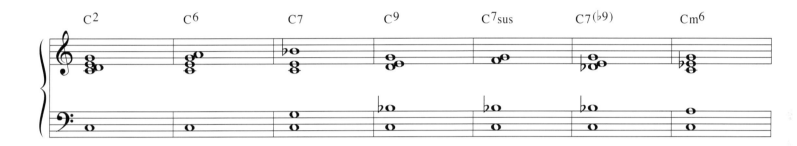

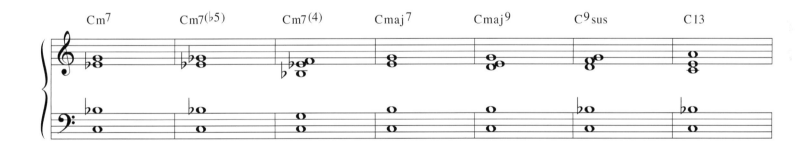

NOTE: Any chord symbol using TWO letter names *separated by a horizontal line* tells you that the lower letter is not the "root" of the chord.

For example:

(F Major chord with a 'G' in the bass)

Modulation Charts

One question frequently asked by church accompanists is: *"How can I modulate from one key to another?"* Probably the best answer is: *"That depends on where you're going!"* First you need to know what key you're modulating *to*... and then think about what the V (or V7) chord in the new key is. It will *always* lead you to the I chord (tonic). This isn't the only way to modulate, but is certainly the best place to start.

The following examples (pp. 108–120) demonstrate how to move *smoothly* from one key to another. The *voicing* of each chord is important to avoid having to change hand position and to avoid parallel motion. The following example will illustrate what I mean.

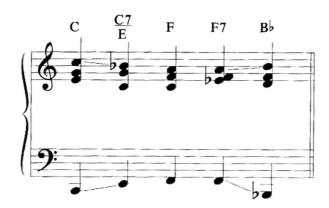

Contrary Motion *and* Common Tones

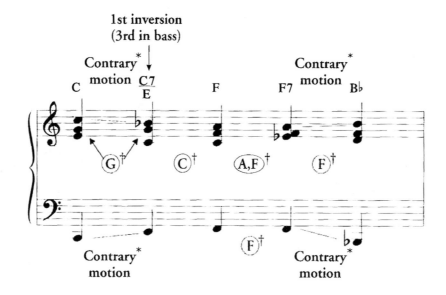

* R.H. moves *lower* as L.H. moves *higher* (and vice versa)
† Indicates *common tone* between two chords

Original Key: C MAJOR

Original Key: Db MAJOR

Original Key: D MAJOR

Original Key: E♭ MAJOR

Original Key: E MAJOR

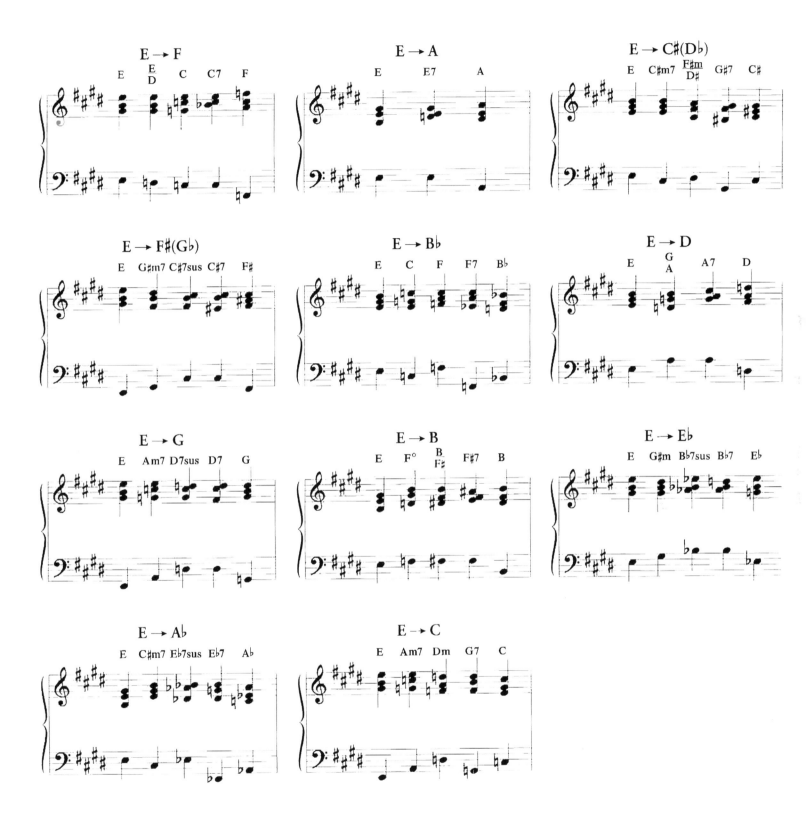

Original Key: F MAJOR

Original Key: G♭ MAJOR

Original Key: G MAJOR

Original Key: A♭ MAJOR

Original Key: A MAJOR

Original Key: B♭ MAJOR

Original Key: B MAJOR